BASS BUILDERS

'70s Funk & Disco Bass

by
Josquin
des Prés

T0045076

To access audio visit:
www.halleonard.com/mylibrary

3495-6717-0580-6134

CONTENTS

Guitar for cover image provided by Cascio Music.

Visit Hal Leonard Online at **www.halleonard.com**

ISBN 978-0-634-02856-4

7777 W. BLUEMOUND RD. P.O. BOX 13819 MILWAUKEE, WI 53213

Introduction

Funk music came about in the mid '60s as an offshoot of R&B. Newly prominent, the electric bass rapidly became the bottom end of popular music. When the style spilled over into the '70s, great bassists like James Jamerson, Anthony Jackson, Bernard Edwards, Larry Graham, Bootsy Collins, Louis Johnson, and Verdine White provided the grooves that sent the world to the dance floor. The disco era was born.

Unlike '80s, '90s, and contemporary dance music, which rely mainly on monotonous, programmed bass patterns, funk and disco bass lines of the '70s were intricate, sometimes complex. Along with the upbeat hi-hat cymbals, the bass played a key role in creating these grooves. Groups like The O-Jays, Kool & The Gang, Graham Central Station, Chic, Sister Sledge, and Earth Wind & Fire (to name just a few) were supported by these pioneering bass players that helped create the disco phenomenon.

I started playing bass in the early '70s. Listening to and learning to play funk and disco bass lines quickly made me understand the importance of "groove" in popular music. Funk music and groove defy traditional music-book study methods—I believe they're better learned by "on the job" training, using your ears and your feel to just *play*. *'70s Funk & Disco Bass* approaches the music from this organic perspective. It does not cover techniques and concepts. There are no exercises, just 101 bass patterns in this style. You go straight into learning how to play the grooves. After all, this is how the bassists who created this style learned to play back in the day! Enjoy.

—*Josquin des Prés*

Recorded and mastered at Track Star Studios, La Mesa, California.
Recording engineer Rolf Doelling, mastering engineer Tristan des Prés

About the Author

*Born in St. Tropez, France, **Josquin des Prés** is a world-renowned bassist who has shared credits with such players as **Jeff Porcaro, Steve Lukather, Vinnie Colaiuta, Billy Sheehan, Bunny Brunel, Jimmy Crespo, David Garibadi, Alex Acuna**, and **Jerry Goodman**, among others. Many of his bass lines can be heard on various loops sample CDs. In addition to his career as a bass player, Josquin des Prés is the author of twelve bass instruction and music reference books, as well as an accomplished producer and songwriter, with credits on over 40 CDs and numerous songs covered by international artists including multiple collaborations with **Elton John's** lyricist, **Bernie Taupin**.*

Pattern 1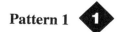

Play 4 times

Pattern 2 2

Play 4 times

Pattern 3 3

Play 4 times

Pattern 4 4

Play 4 times

Pattern 5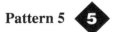

Play 4 times

Pattern 6 6

Play 4 times

Pattern 7 7

Play 4 times

Pattern 8 8

Swing feel

Play 4 times

Pattern 9

Play 4 times

Pattern 10

Play 4 times

Pattern 11

Play 4 times

Pattern 12

5

Pattern 13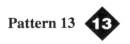

Play 4 times

Pattern 14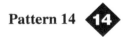

Play 4 times

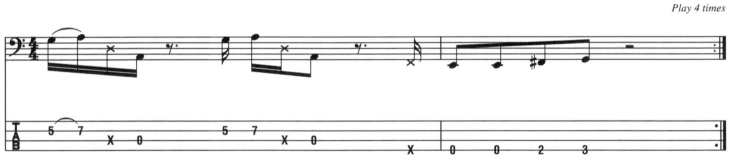

Pattern 15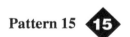

Play 4 times

Pattern 16

Play 4 times

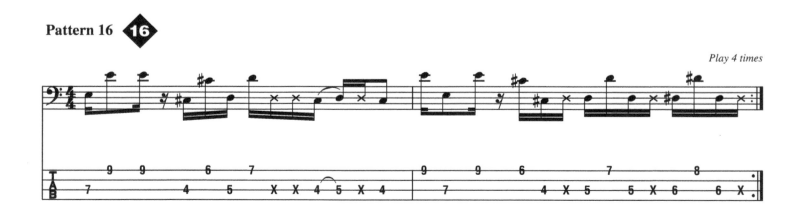

Pattern 17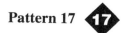

Play 4 times

Pattern 18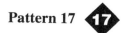

Play 4 times

Pattern 19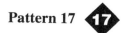

Play 4 times

Pattern 20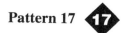

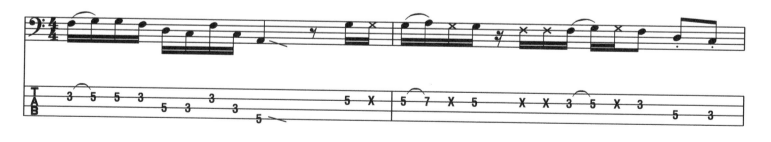

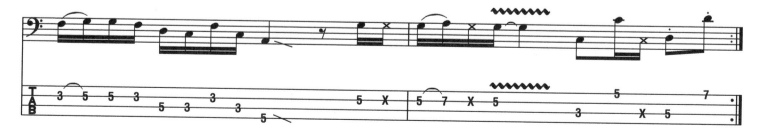

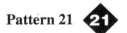
Play 4 times

Pattern 22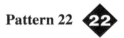

Play 4 times

Pattern 23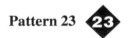

Play 4 times

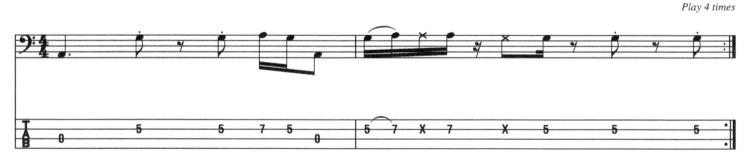

Pattern 24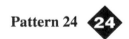

Play 4 times

Pattern 25

Play 4 times

Pattern 26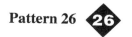

Play 4 times

Pattern 27 27

Pattern 28

Pattern 29

Play 4 times

Pattern 30

Play 4 times

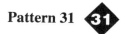

Pattern 32

 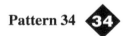

Play 4 times

 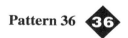

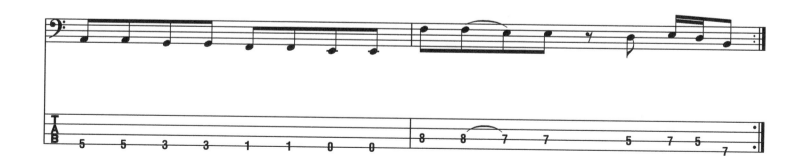

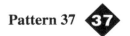

Pattern 37

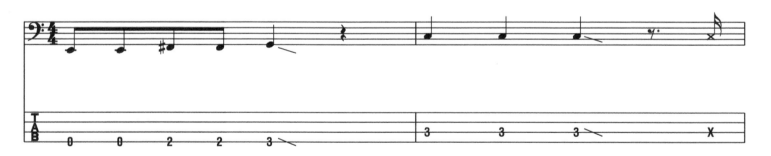

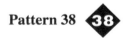

Pattern 38

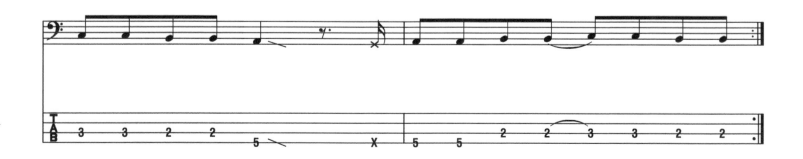

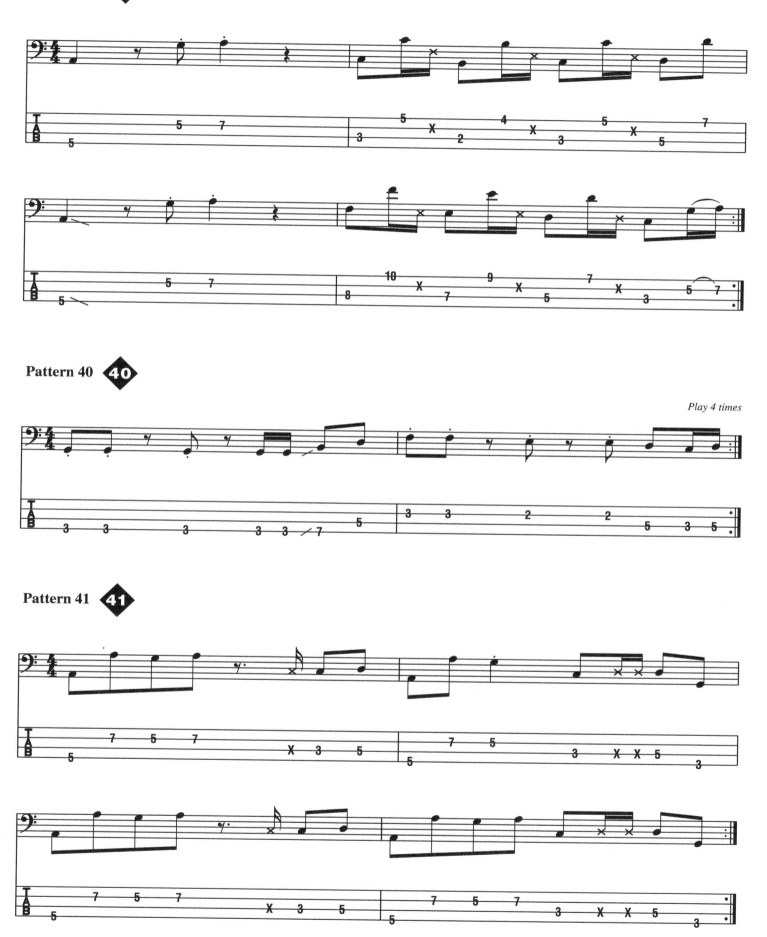

Pattern 42

Play 4 times

Pattern 43

Play 4 times

Pattern 44

Play 4 times

Pattern 45

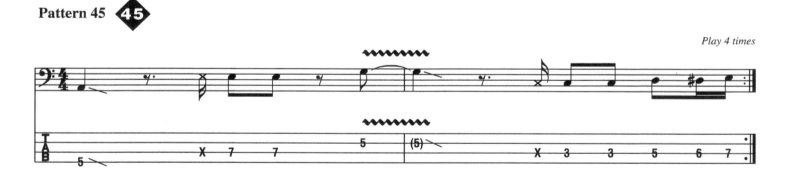

Play 4 times

Pattern 46

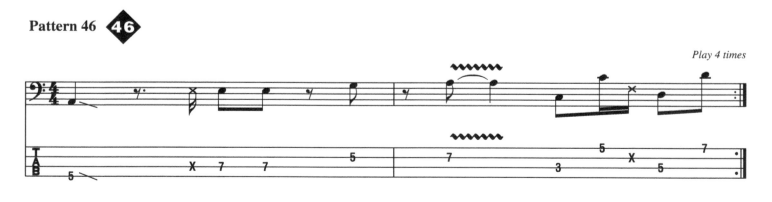

Play 4 times

Pattern 47

Play 4 times

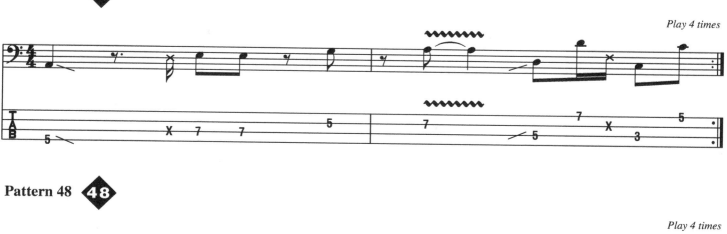

Pattern 48 48

Play 4 times

Pattern 49 49

Play 4 times

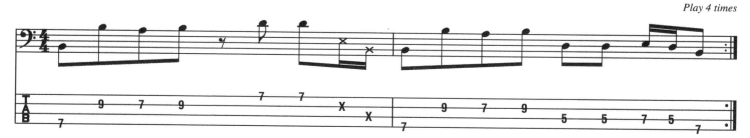

Pattern 50 50

Play 4 times

Pattern 51 51

Play 4 times

Play 4 times

Pattern 53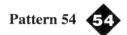

Pattern 54 54

Play 4 times

Play 4 times

Pattern 56

Play 4 times

Pattern 57

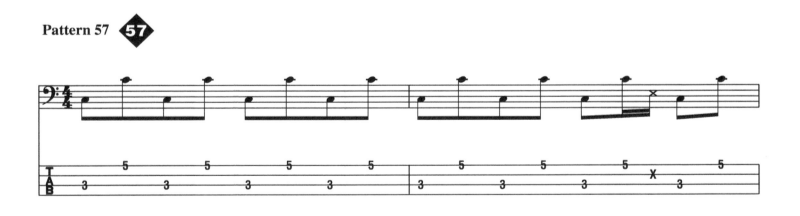

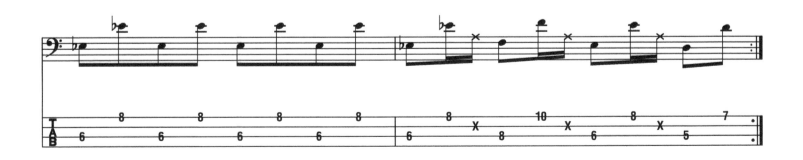

Play 4 times

Pattern 59

Play 4 times

Pattern 60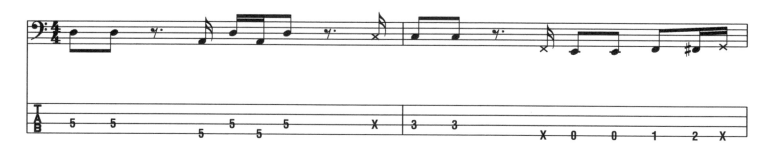

Pattern 61

Play 4 times

Pattern 62

Pattern 63

Pattern 64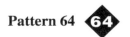

Pattern 65 65

Play 4 times

Pattern 66 66

Play 4 times

22

Pattern 67 67

Play 4 times

Pattern 68 68

Play 4 times

Pattern 69 69

Play 4 times

Pattern 70 70

Play 4 times

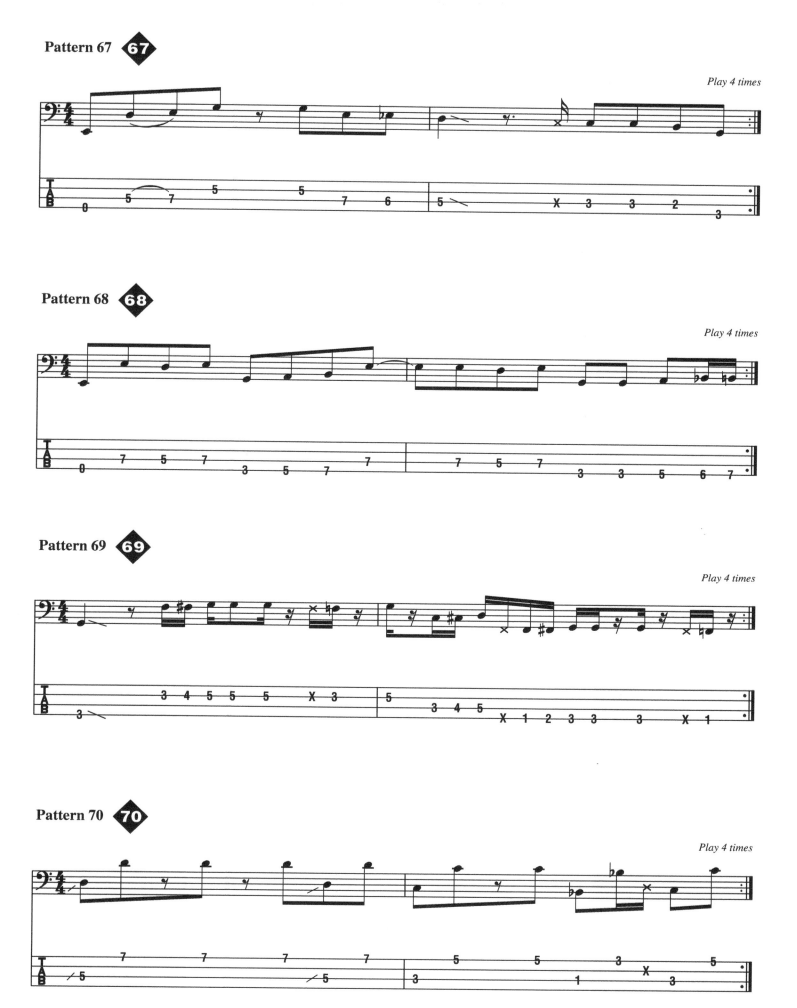

Pattern 71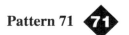

Pattern 72

Pattern 73

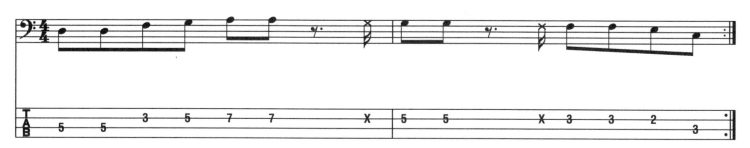

Pattern 74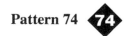

24

Pattern 75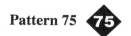

Pattern 76 76

Pattern 77 77

Pattern 78

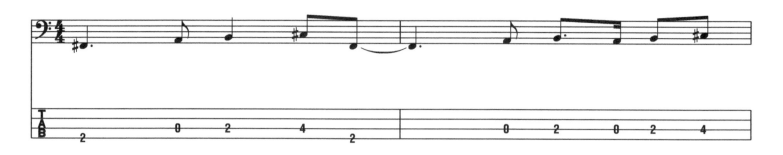

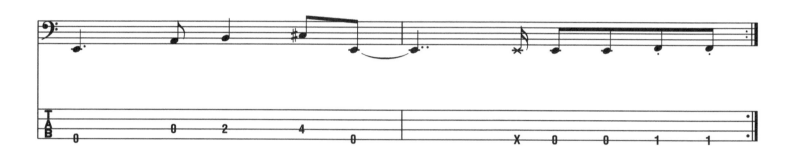

Pattern 79

Play 4 times

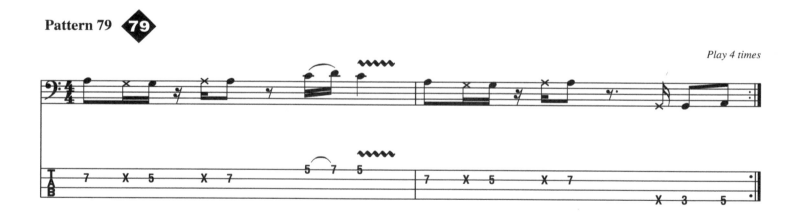

Pattern 80

Play 4 times

Pattern 81

Play 4 times

Pattern 82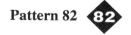

Play 4 times

Pattern 83

Play 4 times

Pattern 84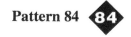

Play 4 times

Pattern 85

Play 4 times

Pattern 86 86

Play 4 times

Pattern 87 87

Play 4 times

Pattern 88 88

Play 4 times

Pattern 89

Pattern 90

Pattern 91

Pattern 92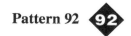

Pattern 93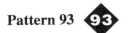

Play 4 times

Pattern 94

Play 4 times

Pattern 95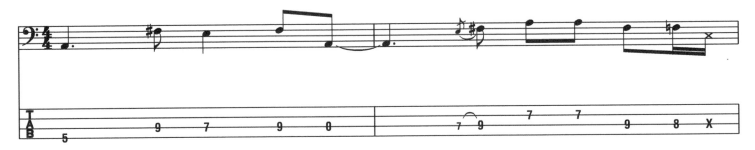

Pattern 96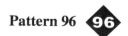

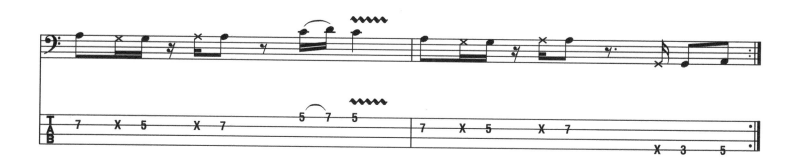

Pattern 97 97

Play 4 times

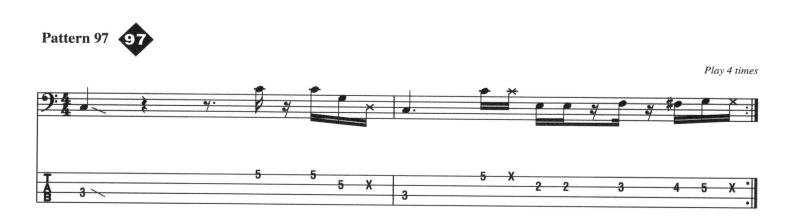

Pattern 98 98

Play 4 times

Pattern 99

Pattern 100 (cont'd)

Play 4 times

Pattern 101 (cont'd)

Play 4 times